—HEELED—
HEARTS

— HEELED —
HEARTS

STEPPING OUT
OF THE HURT

GABRIELLA DENT

PALMETTO
PUBLISHING
Charleston, SC
www.PalmettoPublishing.com

Copyright © 2023 by Gabriella A. Dent

All rights reserved.

No portion of this book may be reproduced, stored in a retrieval system, or transmitted in any form by any means–electronic, mechanical, photocopy, recording, or other–except for brief quotations in printed reviews, without prior permission of the author.

Paperback ISBN: 979-8-8229-3092-6

*Stepping out of the hurt of physical,
mental, and emotional abuse.
Hoping to give someone else support so
that they, too, can make it through.*

Physical Abuse: To use something for the purpose of causing harm; to misuse. To treat an animal or person with cruel or violent expression, especially in a repeated pattern. Cruel or violent treatment through the use of words, objects, or bodily injury.

Emotional Abuse: Emotional abuse is something that we all go through at some point in our lives. Sometimes we even become victims of this without even realizing that we have been hurt until the behavior is continued repeatedly. It can be in the form of verbal intimidation, being isolated, yelling, insults, or a loss of self-worth. Something hurts on the inside that makes us feel unsure, a feeling we sometimes don't know how to handle. Emotional abuse is said to be the hardest to deal with.

Mental Abuse: This is very similar to emotional abuse, where a victim can go into depression, experience stress, have suicidal thoughts, or want to hurt themselves or others.

Abuse is not something easy to deal with, or to talk about. There is help. Get help, even if it means just communicating with someone that you trust.

If you know someone who needs help, or if you are a victim of any form of abuse and would like help or speak to someone, please call the National Domestic Violence Hotline at (800)799-7233, available 24-7, 365 days a year, or contact your local authorities.

Part 1

INTRODUCTION:
YOU ARE NOT ALONE

Today, I lay as I have done many days before and thought about my life, my struggles, my accomplishments, my children, my goals, my upbringing, my skills, my education, talents, hobbies, and my financial situation, and what I can do to improve all of it. They say one will know when they are tired, when they have had enough, when they want more, and when they are not feeling complete, also when they are not feeling accomplished, and not the person who they know that they are and can be. Well today, I am that one. I know what I want, need, dream of, am capable of, and most of all I know what my strengths are. Today, I'm stepping out on faith and doing something instead of settling for something. Today, I embrace who, and what, I am about to become in helping those that are like me. Today is the day that the hearts that were once broken learn to be free, be heard, and begin to heal.

These stories are about picking up one's self after an abusive relationship. Abuse can be mental, physical, and emotional. It can cause a person to fall deeply into depression; it can cause loved ones to take their own lives as well as causing someone to lose theirs. Being abused is NOT okay. If you are a victim, please seek help, tell someone. Victims of abuse are not easy at times to recognize, but if you know someone who is, please be the aid that they need toward a healthy life. I lost a small percentage of my hearing and have terrible lifelong back pain due to my abuse. I am lucky to be alive, and I'm thankful that I can now reach out and help someone else.

This writing is dedicated to my children, and all of the children who have been through, seen, or have lost someone who has been hurt through abuse, whether physical, mental, or emotional. To all the women who have burdened the hurt of pain from abuse, and to all the men who silently have been abused. Special thanks to all my family members who have continually encouraged me and supported my efforts.

I want to share some of my experiences as well as stories others have shared as we travel down the path of healing. There will be obstacles, people who will stand in your way and doubt you, they will doubt your stories and your testimonies. There will be strangers who will lift you up, hug you, inspire you, and encourage you. Just know that you will be the one to take the steps, shed the tears as you tell your story, smile at where you are now, and push forward to a better place in life. Please don't give up on you. Continue to fight, continue to believe, continue to be a listening ear to those who come to you with their stories of hurt, continue to seek help, guidance, and continue to love yourself and others. This journey will not be easy. It will be painful, but I guarantee not as painful as the harm you once experienced while going through the actual hurt. HEAL your hurt, HEAL your HEART. Don't be afraid anymore; you are not alone, you are strong, and you are beautiful.

These short stories, which have been intentionally shortened so as not to expose you, the reader, to more hurt, and the short poetry between the stories are to encourage you, and let you know you can be healed, you are beautiful, you are loved. Get up and put your heels on. Wash the dishes in heels, watch television in heels, pick up your children in heels, take yourself to lunch in heels, do all the things you enjoy in your new healed heels. I love you all, and thank you for allowing me to help you HEEL YOUR HEART. Go ahead, STEP OUT OF THAT HURT!

*Dedicated to my mother, RIP Carmina J. Gillard.
Your eyes have seen so much of what I went through, your ears have heard the pain that silently lay within me, and your hands have dried the tears and rubbed the aches of my body when I needed you to. You would have been proud of me as I now stand stronger than ever, telling others of my hurt.*

You are missed and loved dearly.

MOMMA, I DIDN'T FORGET

The love you gave me

The tears you wiped

The answers you showed me on how life really could be.

I didn't forget the day you gave me my very own doll. No I didn't forget

I didn't forget the afternoon walks and the late-night talks and your laughter like no other.

 I didn't forget the unexpected gifts and special dinners

I didn't forget the love, warmth, or the person who was always there when I needed her the most

I didn't forget...YOU.

Written by your daughter, Gabriella

SHE WAS ONLY SIXTEEN

Innocence graced the eyes of Lisa Bailey, a beautiful young sixteen-year-old girl born and raised in the beautiful Caribbean Islands. Lisa, who is a great athlete, scholar, and captain of her high school's BETA club, had this huge crush on one of her classmates named Desmond. Desmond Taylor, tall, good looking, the starriest hazel eyes you can imagine. He was popular among many of the high school girls because of his ability to bring happiness in any room that he entered. He was known as the class clown, the entertainer, the one person who seemed to take nothing serious, that one person everyone wanted to be around.

During an assembly, Lisa sat across the bleachers where she would have a good glimpse of Desmond as he made all the students around him giggle and swivel in their seats because of something he said. Lisa started giggling herself, as if she could hear what the jokes were that he was telling. It wasn't until someone elbowed her to tell her to be quiet that she realized what she was doing. At the end of the assembly as everyone else was leaving, Lisa sat there gazing at every move Desmond made. She jumped as she heard her name echoing throughout the auditorium. "Lisa," her friend Ina, was calling her. "Girl, didn't you hear me calling you? I know what you were doing, you're daydreaming about that fool Desmond again, aren't you?" Lisa just smiled as she and Ina left the auditorium.

Later that week in science class, Lisa got the nerves up to say something to Desmond, hoping he didn't embarrass her by laughing or calling her out in front of the other students. She finally got the nerves to tell him that she liked him and thought they should meet up on the weekend after the big track meet. Desmond agreed, and Lisa walked away smiling from ear to ear. When Saturday came around, Lisa met Desmond in the gym as they had agreed, and they went to the movies. After the movies, Lisa wanted to get something to eat. She asked Desmond if he minded if they stopped at the twenty-four-hour local diner. Desmond didn't respond, but then instead looked at Lisa like she had done something wrong. "What? Did I say something wrong?" she asked him. "I know you have got to be hungry too, we've been at the stadium all day, and after that long movie, I'm starving." Desmond didn't even bother to pull the car over. Before she knew it, Lisa felt a burning on the side of her face. Desmond had slapped her so hard that she couldn't even say anything as she sat there in shock. "What's wrong with you?" she asked him. "You hit me. I thought we were having a great time. Besides, you're one of those men that like to hit on girls? I did not see that in you. Please take me home."

Desmond pulled up at a gas station, turned to Lisa, and once again hit her so hard that this time she was bleeding from the corner of her mouth. "Look!" he shouted. "You are not my girlfriend, and if you wanted something to eat, you should have gotten it at home. Get out of my car." Lisa grabbed her backpack and got out of the car. She stood there crying, wondering how she would get home. An hour later, Lisa was home after she walked all the way, afraid of calling anyone because she was so embarrassed and didn't know how to explain what had happened to her.

Monday morning at school, Lisa saw Desmond at the lockers and went over to him and asked him why he did what he had done. "Get out my face, stupid," he yelled. Everyone looked at her as she felt the embarrassment that she dreaded all along before she even talked to him last week.

"Desmond, why are you talking to me like that?" she built up the nerves to say.

Before she could get a response, Desmond grabbed her and pushed her against the locker. "Look, I told you to get out of my face."

Lisa jerked away from him and ran down the hallway crying. She ran to the closest room, and she saw it was the art room where one of the teachers was preparing for her class, but Lisa didn't even notice that she was there.

"Are you okay?" Lisa didn't even realize anyone was in the room; she just wanted to get away from Desmond.

"Ah, um, yes, I'm okay," Lisa responded.

Ms. Walker walked over to her and saw the bruise around her eyes from the previous hit on Saturday, and looked Lisa in the eye. "So are you going to tell me the truth about what happened to your face?"

Not having anyone to talk to, and not knowing what to say, Lisa said, "No, I'm not. There is nothing to explain." Lisa turned and walked away.

A few days later, Lisa, her mother, her cousin Asia, and her little sister were all sitting watching the evening news when they heard that a young man had gotten arrested for beating up a student at the same school Lisa attended. Lisa looked up and saw that it was Desmond, and the girl was her friend Ina. Ina went out with Desmond that night, not knowing that Lisa had done the same a few days earlier, and Desmond beat her up so badly that she had to be hospitalized. Lisa got up and ran out of the room. Her mother went behind her and stopped her just before she got a chance to close her door. "Isn't that the same boy you went out with the other night? And is that how you got that bruise on your face you think I did not see?" She didn't even give herself a chance to respond before Lisa grabbed her mother around the waist and cried so hard until her legs were weak. They sat on the bed as her mother told her that she loved her, that she was beautiful, and she was worth more than anything that Desmond or any man like him could do for her. In her heart Lisa hurt more than anyone would understand because she really liked Desmond for a long time. She believed that with her help he would be a good person.

The numbers on the door read room 358, bed A. The room number where Ina was hospitalized. Lisa entered the room and saw her friend lying there all bruised up. She leaned over the bed and kissed Ina on the forehead. "I am so sorry," Lisa cried as she told Ina about her night out with Desmond. "If only I had told you about it, you would not have given that fool the time of day."

"It's okay," Ina said. "He's got what's coming to him. The question is, where do we go from here? How do we heal from this? Who can we talk to? Lisa, I'm okay, please don't cry," Ina said through the wires that held her jaw together. "Hold my hands. Let's pray for us and for Desmond, that he gets the help that he needs. And when I'm out of here, you and I are gonna talk about this..." Both the girls laughed, then prayed.

The End

Remember, a walnut has curves and deep grooves on its outside, but when cracked open, it is as beautiful as one can imagine. You are beautiful inside and out. You are strong enough to make it out alive.

—*Gabriella*

Where Did They Go from Here? How Did They Use Their Hurt?

Desmond spent three days in a juvenile detention center for beating on Ina. He was later placed on probation for six months. It was said that he was in several different relationships where he had beaten other young ladies. No one else ever pressed charges against him.

Ina continued her education and attended a university in Maryland, where she is studying to become a high school counselor.

Lisa moved to a nearby town, continued her education, and today helps young women in a support group to learn to love themselves before they allow others to tell them what love should look like, and how to identify some signs of abuse. Lisa and Ina continue to be great friends.

Story of a friend, written by Gabriella A. Dent, author.

Self-Journal

What do I do with my hurt?

POWDER

It was a beautiful Sunday morning, and here in Florida, one of the things that everyone likes to do is spend time on the beach. Why not? The weather is usually beautiful, the beach will most likely be crowded with lots of people, and staying home is not the thing to do in this area on a Sunday. Margaret made sure that she got up early to do all her chores and got her sons, Matt and Bailey, ready for the day. The excitement was so high; everyone was eager to spend the day with the rest of the family. The phone rang, and the voice on the line was Terry, Margaret's older brother. "Hey sis, we will see you today, right? You haven't shown up the last three times we all planned on going to the beach. Besides, it's been a while since I got a chance to beat you in a game of dominoes. Haha," he laughed through the phone.

"Yes, I am planning on being there. The kids are all ready to go, I just have a few more things to get cleaned up before the mister gets home—you know how he likes things in order."

"Okay then, just hurry up, we will be there in about an hour. Hey sis, I'll have your chair ready for you. I love you."

"I love you too," she replied.

Margaret was finally finished with all the things she had lined up for the day. She decided to wear her pink floral swimsuit with a pair of white shorts and some strappy sandals. She picked out a wide-brim straw hat and a clear, see-through big bag for her towels and trinkets. "Mom, we are ready, what's taking you so long?"

"I'm almost ready too, hold on, the beach isn't going anywhere. I have to call your dad to let him know we are going. I forgot to mention it to him earlier."

"Ahh man, not again, you forgot the last time. He's going to be mad at you again."

"He'll be fine, it's only the beach," she replied. Margaret knew that her son was right; Doug was going to be upset. She sat on the bed as she contemplated what she was going to say when she called.

The phone rang, interrupting her thoughts. It was Doug. "Hey babe, how are you? How's your day going so far?"

She quickly paused, took a deep breath, then said, "I'm fine, what's with all the questions?"

"I know you are not planning on going to the beach with your family today, right? Because you know how I feel about you going out there, showing all your body to everyone."

"Doug, you know you have nothing to worry about. The kids haven't been to the beach in a long time, and it would be nice to take them. I did everything around the house already, and I made dinner early so we can all have dinner when we get back."

"So you were already planning on going, I see?"

"Come on, babe, it's not that big of a deal."

Doug burst out in sarcastic laughter in a tone that Margaret knew all too well. She had heard it many times before. She began to feel a bit nervous, not knowing what was coming next. "So tell me," Doug said, "How are you planning to leave the house? You know if I see any footprints on the powder that I put on the floor, it's going to be some problems."

"You put powder on the floor again? Our children can't spend all their time in the house. It's the weekend, for goodness' sake. I am going to the beach, Douglas, I already told my family that I would be there. I promise we won't be long, a couple of hours at the most. We will be back before you get home."

Silence filled the lines as Margaret said, "I love you, Doug," and hung up the phone. Later that evening when Margaret and the children got back from the beach, Margaret was worried, but felt it would only be an argument when she got in. To her surprise, Doug grabbed her by her hair before she could even enter the house completely. He dragged her into the room, and all you could hear was her yelling, "Doug, stop, stop hitting me, Doug, please." Moments later Doug came out of the room. Margaret followed a few minutes later. He went outside to get the children out of the car; Margaret had told them to stay in the car while she went ahead of them to see what kind of mood Doug was in. Doug acted as if nothing had happened. He asked the children a line of questions. "Who all was at the beach? Did Mommy talk to anyone besides her family? Did Mommy go for a swim with anyone besides them?" Both the children just sat there scared. Doug yelled at them and they began to cry. Margaret ran outside thinking he was hitting them. She grabbed her oldest son by the hand and picked up the younger one, taking them into the house. Margaret got the children ready for dinner as tears continually ran down her face.

"Mommy, are you okay? Mommy, are you mad with us too?"

"No, I am not," she responded. "I'm okay. Daddy is just upset we went to the beach, but it will be okay."

Later that night as everyone completed dinner and the kitchen was cleaned, Margaret went into the bedroom and wrote yet another journal entry of her abuse. She had so many stories and dates jotted down that she planned on one day sharing with someone. "What am I going to do?" she began to write. "I can't do this much longer. I need to get out." Those were the words she wrote as she placed her pen in between the pages. She sat there numb, speechless, puzzled at what she needed to do to protect herself and her children. Who can she call and talk to? Who would even listen? Better yet, who would believe? Everything seemed so perfect around her, in her home. "No one will ever believe me," she wrote as she closed her journal.

> *Be still and know that I am God.*
> —Psalm 46:10

In all things be patient, prayerful, and know that the ending will bring new life. God is working things out for you.

Margaret finally left Doug. Through her journaling she has learned to open up and speak up about her feelings. Doug was mentally abusing Margret by belittling her, and at times he would hit her. Instead of letting it completely break her down, Margaret has been attending counseling with Doug to help them build a better relationship. She has also been personally confiding in her pastor at church, seeking God's guidance toward her healing. Turns out, Doug was verbally abused by his parents and some family members. Communication was not something he learned how to express himself. Margaret did not give up on him; she loved him, but she had to do what was best for her children. Her prayers and her faith have allowed them to heal together. Though things are not perfect, together with prayer and a stronger faith, each day gets a little bit better.

Self-Journal

What are some ways that you have learned to communicate with others, allowing for positive outcomes?

HOW DARE YOU?

What a beautiful day. Everyone's laughing, combing each other's hair, and enjoying our time bonding as sisters. Out of nowhere a sudden scream. He pushed past everyone and got to where Sharon was. No one realized what was happening at first. Randy, Sharon's boyfriend, hit her so hard as he screamed out all types of name-calling and offensive words to her, what seemed like a million profanities. He was beating on her while her sisters tried to help her. After he had been hitting on her for a few minutes, he was gone as quickly as he came in. The highway was close enough, and the counties were even closer. "Someone please get help, call the cops before he gets away."

Away he did. By the time the police came, Sharon was left beaten and bruised. "There is nothing we can do, being that he may already be in the next county," said one of the cops. Haven't we heard this one before?

Sharon was young and in love with the man she felt would be her soulmate. She was visiting with family on a beautiful, carefree day. In her mind she knew that she was gone too long and her time would have to come to an end soon from visiting them. The energy within the home was so flavorful that she simply lost track of time. Randy, the man that clearly did not love her the way she thought he would, had once again left his mark on her face. Sharon never told her family how bad the abuse was, nor how often it took place. How dare he? How could he just barge in like that? Who does he think he is? Lord, you have got to get me out of this relationship for good. Those were the words that Sharon played in her mind over and over. What will it take for her to be free from the hands that once held her in love, but now hurt her? Show me a way out before it's too late for me.

She arrived home after several hours at the hospital due to the incident. Sharon did not know what to do. She was so afraid that Randy would beat her up again, and this time there would be no one there to help her. Slowly she walked into the narrow doorway of the apartment, walking soft and slow. What is going to happen to me? I can't take another hit, I'm weak, hurting, and I need to clean my face up from the earlier beating. Lord, my life is in your hands. Sharon walked through every room of the apartment and realized after a while that Randy wasn't even at home. She fell to the floor of her kitchen and cried hard and long. She was crying so hard that she was getting out of breath. A sigh of relief came over her as she just laid there, weak. She began to doze off from crying so much when she caught herself and decided to go take a warm shower to soothe her body. A few hours later, she heard the jingling of keys and knew Randy was home. She had time to calm down and get her thoughts together.

On the inside, she was shaking like a leaf, but the words that came out of her mouth made her feel strong. "Randy, how dare you hit me in front of my family? It's bad enough that you do this at home for no reason, but now you are doing it in front of others." Sharon was expecting another hard hit to her face, but Randy just pushed past her mumbling words she couldn't understand. Once he was gone, Sharon sat on the sofa in disbelief that she had stood up to him and he just walked away. Sharon said a silent prayer thanking God for the strength and the words that he passed upon her lips. She fell asleep on the sofa without any worries. The next morning, she awakened and went into the room. Randy was gone. Should I call him? she said to herself. No, why should I? I hope he stays gone. An hour later, as Sharon entered the kitchen, she found a small piece of used paper with writing on the back. It said, "I'm sorry. I thought you were leaving me again because you stayed away so long. I hope that you are here when I get home from work. I love you, Randy." What? I'm sure you are sorry. Sharon said out loud. How many times is he going to say sorry for the same things that he keeps doing? she said to herself. She balled up the paper and threw it in the trash.

Sharon packed all her things and left a note on the bed that said, "I'm sorry, I will not be here when you get back. I can't do this anymore."

A few weeks went by without hearing from Randy. This was really unusual. It would take him about a day or two to come looking for her each time she left. Sharon looked up and stretched her arms out and said, "Thank you, Lord, for loosening my shackles." Sharon felt that maybe Randy had gotten the message clear that you can't keep hurting the person you love. She never heard from him again, until one day she saw his sister and she stated that he was sick. God has a way of making a way, she thought. She said, "Tell him I said to pray. He needed help," and walked away.

The End

We tend to allow others to dictate our happiness, to dictate how we should behave and who we can socialize with, when we are in an abusive relationship. It's not easy fighting back or trying to get away, as some may think. It's easy for others to judge and say, "Why do you stay?" or "Why do you keep going back?" Trust me, it's not that at all. There is this thing called fear that will hold you hostage in situations that you don't want to be in. Fear will make you feel insecure, lost, ugly, and weak. Fear will leave you hopeless. When that happens, it's easy to stay.

In life we have to find a way to make the choices that will give us strength and allow us to live a happier, healthier life. It may take longer to leave, but have a plan of escape so that you won't go back. I found help through a friend, who later became my husband, and I never looked back. Was I scared? Yes, every move I made, I looked over my shoulder wondering if my abuser would find me. I didn't go to many places besides church, work, or visits with family members. As the years went by, things became a little easier to deal with. I still saw the man who hurt me from time to time on the streets as I went about my daily routine. My heart skips a beat, and I get nervous from the flashbacks when I see him. But I know those days are gone. I'm protected by the blood of Jesus. He saved me from that pain, and I'm free to live again, love again, trust again, and be healed.

The End

SHE NEEDS TO KNOW

She didn't know you saw her crying when she did

She didn't know if you heard her when she wept

She thought she was the only one that felt the pain,

The shame, the loss, the grief

How will she make it? Were the notes you saw her write written with pain?

However, will she be able to learn to find the way out, the will to fight?

How will she ever find the will to stand, the will to survive?

There are reasons to the things that she feels,

the things she fears, the things you don't hear

Reasons to the things she holds...within because of fear

One day soon the words she will hold on to will be

YOU ARE FREE!

Go, run, don't look back, don't hide...anymore

It's time for us to tell her why she could, why she should, and that she will

MAKE IT

She really needs to know she's not alone; she is strong, beautiful, and worth it.

SHE HAS WON! She can love, laugh, and LIVE again.

THE CANAL

What a beautiful day to visit with family. Janet was so excited to spend the day babysitting for her cousin, who had asked her to help out a few days before. Being that she doesn't get to see them too often, Janet was ready and willing to help keep the children. Janet had children of her own and thought it would be good to spend time with them. She was right. Her boys played so well with their cousins. They played outdoors so well together, building things from pieces of sticks they found, and building anything that their little imaginations could come up with.

Three days passed by so fast. Janet hated to leave, and so did the children. She called her live-in boyfriend, Larry, to come and get them as he said he would. As she waited with the children, a young man knocked on the door. He was about fifteen years old. The young man was pulling a lawn mower and had a rake tied on the handle. It was clear that he was going door to door asking all the neighbors if he could cut their lawn. As Janet was addressing his questions, Larry showed up. From the look on his face, she could see that he was angry. Without any questions, Larry hurriedly got out of the car, rushed to the door, and pushed the young man out the way. He burst through the door of the house and started hitting on Janet. She could hear the children crying and screaming and other people, who she thought were the neighbors and family members, yelling at him to stop. Why was he doing that? And to get out of the house. The beating was so hard to Janet's face and body that all she could try to do was to protect her face as much as possible with her hands. That was not helping. Before long she felt blood running down her face. Her eyes were swollen and she could hardly see. Larry continued to hit on her viciously. He dragged her outside and continued the beating.

There was a canal at the back of the house. He proceeded to try to drag Janet to the backyard in that direction. She yelled, screamed, and tried her best to get away. Larry kept telling her he was going to kill her because she was cheating right in front of him. He thought that the young man at the door was leaving the house, not knowing he was trying to do business. Janet vaguely remembered who but felt someone pulling her legs to stop Larry from dragging her to the canal. Someone yelled, "We called the police!" "Leave her alone," "You are going to beat her to death." By that point Janet was weak and nearly passed out. Larry finally stopped when he heard the sirens coming. He ran to his car and left in the opposite direction of the sirens. He got away, again.

Separated by a major highway were two county lines. Because of that, the local police could not do anything to Larry after he crossed county lines. Janet was taken to the local hospital badly beaten and couldn't recall everything that happened when the police questioned her. Her mother came to the hospital, in tears and defenseless as she held Janet's hands as she cried. Janet remembered hearing the doctor telling her mother that she, Janet, could not keep getting abused like this or he might not be telling her to take her daughter home, but that she didn't make it. Janet cried silently hearing those words and knew that she had to get out of that relationship. She cried and prayed, asking God to help her, show her the way, send her the help she needed to get out of that abusive relationship alive. She had to get out for herself and for her children.

Janet was discharged a few hours later. She went home to her mother's house. Three weeks and four days later, after several phone calls and threats if she didn't come back, along with promises never to do it again, Janet went back to Larry. He was very apologetic and proclaimed his love for her. The daily beatings that she previously received seemed to have ended. Janet knew that she didn't love Larry anymore, but because she was afraid he would do the horrible things he said if she didn't come back, or hit her again, she returned to him. During her time back home with Larry, Janet began to stash as much money as she could and talk to as many people as she could about where to get help without him finding her. She started packing a getaway bag for her and the children. She made up her mind that she would leave Larry—she just had to be careful planning it. She continued to cook, clean, and keep things as peaceful as possible until the day she was ready to finally leave. She knew it would happen again; she just didn't know when. A few weeks after that, while at work, Janet's mother introduced her to a coworker of hers. Janet was not interested in meeting anyone else. She was still planning her escape from Larry, and the last thing she needed was to be accused of seeing someone else, especially since she didn't know him. She didn't want to have to tell her story to anyone. That was the last thing on her mind. How could she love again? A stranger at that. How could she find a man to love her? After all, Larry constantly told her she was not beautiful, that no man would want a woman with so many children, that she would come back to him every time she left. Larry's voice rang loudly in her head as she began speaking to this stranger. I guess if my mother thinks he's a good man, then I should open up and see what happens, Janet thought silently. After a few days communicating with her new friend, Janet began telling him her story little by little. She did not want to scare him away. It was nice having someone to talk to that made her smile. He assured her that she would never have to go through that kind of hurt again, especially with him. Could this stranger be her help that she prayed for to get out of this abusive relationship? Janet was told by him to be ready on a certain day. They were going to meet at a local park she often visited with her children so that they could talk more and have him meet her children. At the park they discussed several things, including the fact that this man was seriously interested in being a part of her life, and that he could help her get away from the abusive relationship. He wanted to help Janet find herself again and protect her. They agreed on a time and place to meet. She was very nervous that she would get caught, but she couldn't wait to get away. Just to get away and smile again, and be loved again, to have a place where she and her children could be safe. Janet still made every day as normal as possible around the house until it was that time for her to take her children and leave. With a burst of new hope, and a fresh start, she was so excited for what was to come. Finally the day came. Janet made dinner, cleaned the house, and left at the time she was told to meet with her children. The doors to the house were kept locked when Larry worked if Janet had no errands to do, which was most of the time. She opened a bedroom window and one by one took her children out to the car as fast as she could before Larry came home. She cried and felt scared that she would get caught.

Every day Janet felt free, but still filled with fear. Every day she cried. She tried to go on with life as best as she could, and with the help of her new support system, she did just that. Weeks, then months, passed by. The tears still came, only this time it was tears of disbelief that she was finally free from the hurt, free from pain, free to love and be loved, free to live. Janet still heard of Larry wondering about her whereabouts from family and friends. She heard that he would call or stalk out their parking lots to see if she was there. She smiled, and said, "He won't find me. I'm free."

WEARY FEET, BEATING HEART

Though the feet get weary
    The heart still beats
Though the sun shines, and the waters flow
In the midst of all this beauty lies a weary feet
and a heart that still beats
Every day given is a gift
Every moment lived is a memory
With every beat, the heart is given new life
From a heart that still beats
Every day someone hurts, every day someone cries
This pain so deep, this weary feet
this pounding heart still beats
Still can beat, still can love, still can be healed
still getting stronger
This heart STILL BEATS

By Gabriella

Self-Journal

*What will it take to keep my heart beating?
I can't give up; I have to survive this.
My heart feels...*

For my children I will...

THE ONE WITHIN, THE REFLECTION

The reflection I see when I look in the mirror, is it really me?

I wonder how much of me is really me? The me that others see

My smile, so defined, leaves an imprint like no other

Some say my smile is like that of my mother...but for this bruise

My voice when I praise him sounds like a heavenly choir, but for this bruise

My laughter so bright used to fill a room

fill every heart with desire to hear the things I had to say, but for this bruise

But does this bruised reflection still say...is it me?

GABRIELLA A. DENT

Is this reflection that I still see me, the me that I see?

This nearly immaculate person that imprisons me

makes me wonder, Who can this be?

As I reflect within this superlative

Looking deep inside to see the me that people see

I see the light, the joy, the happiness within the mind,

the heart and all the paralysis that others see in me

This reflection is truly me!

I love the me that I see, well rounded and full of life

Now can you see the bruised...me that I see?

Self-Journal

What do you see?
Write your own poetry to your healed self.

BROWN EYES BLUED

"Shiny eyes," "bright eyes," "beautiful eyes," those compliments never seem to dull my day. Everywhere I went someone always seemed to compliment me on my eyes. It made me happy. I love wearing my makeup, eyeliner just right, and a bold eye shadow to coordinate with whatever color I was wearing that day. I came to life every time I stepped in front of the mirror. I love my eyes.

This day was different. I found myself patting hunks of foundation around my eyes. No eyeliner today, I told myself. My eyes were too puffy to apply it. The tears flowing down my face made it difficult to get the foundation to stay in place. I wouldn't be able to explain this bruised eye to anyone again. I told my friends and family that this would never happen to me again, but it did. I kept recalling what happened the night before. It was as if it just happened all over again.

I was trembling on the inside, full of fear, afraid to step back into the bedroom. He came home angry again, and I knew better than to ask him what was wrong. But I did. That would only enrage him even more. I was in the living room folding up the laundry that I had washed earlier that day. The children were asleep on the sofa. I had two children and was five months pregnant with my third child. I was young and in love with this man, who couldn't seem to cherish the gifts that he had before him. I hurried to carry the basket of laundry back into the bedroom. As soon as I sat it on the chair, I heard him screaming my name. Afraid to answer, I barely opened my mouth trying to get the words, which finally burst from my mouth.

I walked out into the living room where he was. I could see from that look on his face that I was about to be his punching bag again for no reason whatsoever. I slowly walked over toward him, guessing I was moving too slow, because he jolted from his seat and slapped me so hard. "Get me a beer," he screamed. "What did you do all day? This place is a mess." I never even bothered to answer him because I knew anything I said would be the wrong thing. I didn't want to upset him anymore, so I simply said nothing. "Just laundry and cared for the kids" were the words I said in my head. He called me all sorts of names, nothing that I hadn't heard before.

His phone rang and I was so happy that it took his attention away from me. As he went outside to take his call. I leaned up against the wall, relieved that this did not turn out like all the other beatings, and the tears started rolling down my face. I feared for the life of my unborn child, and the safety of my two sons. I looked out the window to see where he was because he was gone for a while. His car was gone. Thank you, Lord. I sat on the sofa and cried, trying not to awaken the children.

Hours went by. By the time he returned, it was late. I went into the kitchen and warmed up his dinner and took it to him as usual, no questions asked. He looked at me with his evil eyes and grinned. He said, "What did you cook?" I told him what was on his plate. He said, "Come closer," and I did as he asked. He said, "Here, you take a bite first. I know you are upset with me for yelling at you earlier, so I want to make sure the food is the same thing you served my children earlier." I took the fork and took a small piece of everything on his plate, then passed it back to him. I just sat there so as not to make him upset. He ate a few bites, and not long after he was passed out on the sofa from the drinking he went out and had earlier. I took the plate away and went to bed. I was grateful that he did not come back too drunk and angry. I was very exhausted, but I found the strength to write down a few lines in my diary.

"Dear diary, today was not as horrible as some of the others I have shared with you. But nonetheless I am still broken inside, looking for a way out of this terrible relationship before it costs me my life or my children's lives. I know I keep saying I will leave him soon, but it's way more difficult than even I can imagine. I am still praying daily for God to send a light through this tunnel. I think I'm going to sleep well tonight, so that's all for now." As I closed my diary, I fell to my knees and said a short prayer, thanking God for making this night more peaceful than most, for the rest he was about to allow me to get, and for the light that he was preparing to shine through my tunnel.

The next morning, it was like nothing ever happened. I made breakfast for him and the children before he went to work and I went on with my day. Who knows what the end of the day would bring. I am just thankful for the peace that was given to me throughout the night.

DEAR DIARY

Dear diary, another day is coming to an end as I look back at where I have come from. I have reflected on the pain, the sleepless nights filled with worry, the helplessness of fear that strangled me, the thoughts of freedom, but most of all the love for my children and myself that I bear within. It has been a long time coming, and somehow I feel free inside. I know it's nothing that I have done for myself but the grace of God that has kept me. I ask myself on several occasions, When will it all end? Is it best that I just end my life myself? Should I just continue to let these blows to my head take me out? Should I commit murder and end it all, thinking at least I ended the hurt? So many times I played out each role in my head. But God, I knew that was not the thing to do. I was always taught to seek God and stay prayerful, though at times I must say that prayer was the last thing on my mind—instead, I was focused on survival. Then I realized that prayer was inevitable. While I prayed for an ending, waiting for a visual outcome in everything I did, God was already working it out for me indirectly through others. Everything I feared no longer became fearful; the person

I feared no longer worried me. I began to look at fear as a challenge. If I felt it, I would find a way to overcome it. The thing I feared most became smaller and easier to deal with. What is it that kept me mentally strangled? The fear of being caught and killed if I left. I had to believe that God had a better plan for my life. I had to realize that he had a purpose for me, and that the work he has placed me on this earth to fulfill was not complete. I believed that what I was going through was just a part of the journey to my destiny. Once I began to believe, I began to live.

Dear diary, you have been there with me all along. You were my outlet, my listening ear, my encouragement, my secret keeper, my companion, and my silence. I made it!! I never thought the day would come when I could write the words to what was once my pain, my reality. I hope that my stories of what I have been through and where I am now help someone else survive this kind of trauma.

Thank you for being there for me, surviving friend, Gabriella

To my readers: I am now working on more of my writing, crafting, and speaking to others in groups and classes, especially youths about abuse and surviving. There is help out there for you. It's not easy to open up and ask for help, or even let others know that yes, I am a victim. Get help. You will have to give up some things, lose some people, relocate, but whatever it will take to survive, do it for yourself, your children, your family. Look to God for strength and direction. Activate that faith within. I love you, and so does the Father above.

Part 2:

STEPPING OUT OF THE HURT

MY ROAD TO OVERCOMING MY HURT

In this section of my book, I share with you a few of my personal testimonials of how I have made it through the pain of the hurt, which is never forgotten, but pushed behind, making room for the happier things in life. It is never easy going through an abusive relationship or marriage. It is never easy to learn to love, forgive, or trust someone again. I must tell you, through my experience, and journey to recovery, that the most important step in healing is forgiveness. In order to heal, in order to move on, in order to allow someone else to get close to your heart, in order to grow, you must forgive. Forgive your abuser, forgive yourself. God forgave us for our sins, so we must forgive those that have done an injustice to us. I pray that this journey of mine will be as encouraging to you as it still is to me as a part of my daily growth.

IT BEGINS HERE:

FORGIVING YOUR ABUSER

Some of you may be saying I have lost my mind. After all the things that he has done, all the pain that he has caused, and all the pain inflicted on our children. I thought about it long and hard, prayed and prayed, picked up the phone and hung it up countless times thinking, Why bother? He doesn't deserve any of the time or thought that I am putting into this. I drove by the last known address endless times and stopped across the street, waiting to see him come out so that I could talk to him. But I was still too angry, and yes, still a little scared. I didn't think I would be after all those years. I stopped wanting to forgive him. I became angry, depressed, and hurt all over again. Although I had loving support and a great family that helped me get through the hurt, I wanted closure, I wanted healing, and I wanted God's continued presence in my life, so I knew I had to forgive him so I could move on.

A few years went by, and I received an inbox on Facebook from my abuser. I was in disbelief, confused, angry, and yet relieved. It took me several days to open the message, and another few days to respond. When I finally decided to respond, I kept it simple, feeling my way around what to say, how to feel, thinking, Lord, is this you telling me it's time to heal, time to move on, time to forgive? But the pain was keeping me from moving on and love again. I knew it was something that I had to do. I was ready to move on, to be free, to heal, to truly love again.

I got married over the years, and though my marriage wasn't perfect, it helped me learn how a good relationship should and shouldn't be. I had learned to love again, trusting someone with my heart, and raising my children as a whole family unit. I didn't mention the email to my husband at the time. It was something that I had to deal with by myself, although I knew that he would be supportive. He knew that I was hurting from my past. After all he was the man that rescued me from the abusive relationship that I was in by loving me and accepting my children as his own.

My children's father, my abuser, once again reached out to me through Facebook Messenger. After a couple of conversations, the conversation of our past relationship came up. He was still in denial about the abuse and had the nerve to even say to me he didn't do the things I was reminding him of. Anger filled me. I smiled on the other end of the messages as I read them, and said to him, "I have the memories, the stories, the medical records, the police reports, and endless witnesses, including some of your family members." I told him never to contact me again because I cannot continue to give him control over my happiness. He became sarcastic and started saying things to me to once again try to hurt me. He still tries to communicate with me, mostly about himself. Thank God I have grown and changed into a better, peaceful person. At the end of the texting, I looked up, and asked God to please forgive me, for I have forgiven him even though he doesn't realize what he has done.

Forgiveness isn't easy, but it is necessary to move on. Forgive your abuser; learn to live again, love again, and be the best you.

> *Bear with each other and forgive one another if any of you has a grievance against someone. For as the Lord forgave you.*
>
> —Colossians 3:13

THE NEXT STEP

Open up your mouth and speak
You can do this! Yes, you can. I know it hurts, you're ashamed, you fear no one will believe you, but it's been so long, you don't want anyone looking at you differently, you don't want to awaken the memories. You are not alone! You must start the healing. Cry if you must, scream, throw what you need to, but SPEAK OUT, TELL YOUR PAIN. You are FREE.

My sister, my daughter, my niece, my friend, my aunt, my cousin, my family, even you, the woman or child reading this, your story can help someone else. Believe me when I tell you that speaking your truth, your story, helps you too. It's a burden lifted off of you. It's you not holding this pain inside any longer. It's you sharing your testimony of being a survivor, so speak. There are family members and friends who have no idea what you have gone through and why you are the way that you are toward certain things. We must speak out for those who no longer can. Someone lost a daughter, a mother, a sister, a friend, but you are here to help heal, to help save a life. Trust me, it won't feel good at first, but you will feel better at the end. Your support system is waiting.

Here's something that I have learned about sharing my story. I did not start to share my stories, or talk about them with those who witnessed my abuse. I waited until after I had forgiven my abuser, and in certain conversations with a few people, I began to share pieces of what I had gone through. I smiled as I was telling my story because I knew that they would cry and feel sorry for me. So I exhibited, to the best of my abilities, a smile. I told myself, look at you now, you are healing. I asked my friends that I shared with, please don't feel sorry for me or my past, but those tears must be for the person that I am today.

Another thing that I learned is that your story is not for everyone. Let God tell you when to share and whom to share with. Once I started speaking about things, I felt some of the pain lifting away. It became easier to speak about it and to see the vision and places God wants me to see. I am now on a mission to help as many women as I can to step out of their hurt and find life again.

So speak. We are listening. We support you.

SHE CRIES...LOUD

Hello!

What is that sound? Who is making that noise? Why can't I see them?

Hello, are you listening to the sounds I make when I can't even speak?

Are you hearing the sound of my pain even if I'm not telling you?

I am speaking, but you're not hearing

Wait, don't touch me there. It hurts, but you wouldn't know that,

so I pull away with a faint smile, pulling down my sleeves.

Hello, I am speaking to you, but you can't help me because you can't hear me.

GABRIELLA A. DENT

I thought I was being too loud,

but then I realized it's the thoughts in my head that are screaming for help

you can't hear me.

Hello, hello please give me your hands so you can pull me out of my thoughts, feelings, and this place of darkness.

Hello, I have something to say...can you hear me?

NOW THE *YOU* YOU FORGOT ABOUT

Now that you have forgiven your abuser, and you have shared your stories, it's time for you to dress yourself. Yes, you have to now wear a smile. Hold your head up, step out in the outfit you placed in the back of the closet, those heels that you bought so long ago—or even the ones that you wanted to purchase, go get them. Girl, you are beginning to look like the you that once was, the better you. Get up out of that mental place of bondage, pain, depression, and step out into that job, career, relationship, and the self that's been waiting to rise within you.

Finding you again is refreshing. The things you gave up, places you were once forbidden to go, and all the family events you missed are in your control. My prayer for you is that you continue to find the you that is hiding on the inside. It may not feel like a familiar place, but it's rewarding. You deserve to be happier. Go back to school, start that business, live. You got this. There are no limits to you being the best you. Know that someone cares, someone loves you, someone is depending on you, you are depending on you. Happy healing.

NO MORE WILL YOU HEAR

Shut up, you're ugly, you're useless, no one else will want you, I hate you, you will never leave me, I will kill you if you try to leave, what're you gonna do, no one will believe you, I know where your family lives, where were you?

Or feel another slap, punch, kick, stomp, drag, or another sleepless night.

You are a Heeled Heart, stepping out of your HURT

I can do all things through Christ who strengthens me.

—Philippians 4:13

Part 3

WORDS THAT HEAL, ENCOURAGE, AND MOTIVATE

You are beautiful

I am so proud of you

I knew you could

I believe in you

Look at you now

You've got this

If you want it, go for it

I am so glad you are here

I can't wait to see you again

Where have you been?

I miss you

Let's go shopping

You are promoted

It's good to see you

I believe in you

Better is waiting on you

You are important to me

Live without fear

It will only get better

God is able

He's got you

Girl, you are stepping in those heels...lol

GABRIELLA A. DENT

Add on more encouraging words:

My sister, my friend, love yourself, not the memory that holds you. I LOVE YOU, I BELIEVE IN YOU! IT'S OVER, STEP OUT OF your hurt and live.

Free Writing—
Let It Out!!

We support you, we are listening

If you know someone who needs help, or if you are a victim of any form of abuse and would like help or to speak to someone, please call the National Domestic Violence Hotline at (800) 799-7233, available 24-7, 365 days a year, or contact your local authorities.

Special thanks to my family, my church family, and my friends for believing and supporting me through this process of healing.

Special dedication to my late son, Sgt. Lewis A. Clay Jr. He encouraged me to finish my writing and wanted the first copy of it. He paid for his copy before I was even finished writing. I didn't finish it before his passing. He was with me in spirit as I completed my writing. He would have been so proud of me. I will love you forever, Lewis. You are always in my heart.

www.ingramcontent.com/pod-product-compliance
Lightning Source LLC
LaVergne TN
LVHW052002060526
838201LV00059B/3787